D1535105

ALL MY HEROES ARE BROKE

POEMS

ARIEL FRANCISCO

C&R Press
Conscious & Responsible

First Edition
1 2 3 4 5 6 7 8 9

Selections of up to two pages may be reproduced without permissions. To reproduce more than two pages of any one portion of this book write to C&R Press publishers John Gosslee and Andrew Sullivan.

Cover Art by Eugenia Loli
Cover Design by Lisa Williams

Library of Congress Cataloging-in-Publication Data

ISBN: 978-1-936196-75-3
LCCN: 2017943778

C&R Press
Conscious & Responsible
www.crpress.org

For special discounted bulk purchases please contact:
C&R Press sales@crpress.org

para mi familia

"I ain't saying that you never had to struggle for a buck or some luck or some love, motherfucker join the club."

—Atmosphere

ALL MY HEROES
ARE BROKE

TABLE OF CONTENTS

I

A VIEW OF THE STATUE OF LIBERTY
FROM THE BROOKLYN BRIDGE

Locks cling to the bridge's facade like piercings,
inscribed with names in marker or lipstick.
Their keys sunken to the bottom of the East River,
combinations lost in the brackish waters of memory.
A man in a black trench coat sells the locks
to passing couples, encourages them to latch
their hearts onto the bridge that's already heavy
with rust. Way out on the jilted water:
the silhouette of a dream-sized woman standing
on a distant corner looks so familiar from this far away—
arm raised to hail a cab that will never come.

7

BEFORE SNOWFALL

French has no word for home.
　　　　　　—Jack Gilbert

I found Baudelaire on a street corner
near Washington Square Park for two dollars
on a flimsy table littered with orphaned books:

a faded, cracked paperback, lavender
as the lingering winter evening that draped
the skyline like a dust jacket, and small enough

to squeeze into a standard sized envelope,
which I did, after scribbling a little note
on the inside cover to a girl back home.

She never got the book, which was in French,
and we never spoke again in any language,
though I always wondered what happened

to the book, probably lost in the dead letter office,
that mass grave of undelivered letters,
moldy packages, and illegible birthday cards.

Still, when winter arrives every year like a janitor
to sweep the fallen leaves, and I'm reminded
of what is lost, I like to imagine

a homeless man fishing my envelope
out of that dropbox on Broadway
before the mailman gets to it,

digging for Christmas cards from grandma
stuffed with cash for her favorite grandkid,
and instead finding Baudelaire.

He clutches the book with ungloved hands
slumping down against the dropbox
in resignation, and flips it open

to my little note, which simply says
tell me, is the snow coming down
on you too? And I imagine him looking up,

his gaze tracing the skyline until it reaches
the grey horizon, thinking of all the nowheres
to go to lay his head down tonight,

saying out loud:
Not yet my friend. Thank goodness,
not yet.

TULIPS IN WINTER

Unblossomed on a windowsill,
white heads bowed in surrender:
ghosts that tremble in the wake
of wrecking balls, that haunt
men in hardhats until the walls
crumble into the dirty slush.
Where are the hands that placed
them on that ledge, waiting
for them to burst open? Soon,
it will all melt into spring—
that is, it will be forgotten.

I KNOW YOU LOVE MANHATTAN BUT YOU SHOULD LOOK UP MORE OFTEN

after Frank O'Hara

That same sky that once delivered a bright
yellow bird at your feet like the morning
paper, a bundle of bloodied feathers
that would have smashed against your head
if you'd been walking just a step faster.
So what if the sun hasn't come out to speak
to you in days? Even under winter's
tightest fist some light still slips through
to you, and isn't that a miracle?

HAVING A RUM AND COKE ALONE

I sit at the end of the bar
so there's only ever one
empty seat next to me—
in this way I limit possibilities
and think it control. Everything
is fine. I turn to the window
whenever someone walks by.
A stranger would call that
paranoia, but I know better.
Finally, the bartender comes up
all smiles, asks if I'm waiting
for someone. *Yeah, you.*

READING KEATS AT FREEMAN STATION

Above the snow-laced platform:
the waning moon's half-turned face,
like the scarfless man whose socks
show through his shoes, raising a bare
fist to his mouth as an express train
tears past the station, smothering his cough—
it doesn't stop here at this hour.

LOOKING DOWN FROM ATOP
THE EMPIRE STATE BUILDING

Such crowds flow through this city—
the tops of their heads like so many
pennies at the bottom of a wishing well
rippling beneath another tossed prayer.

READING LORCA AT UNION SQUARE

Asesinado por el cielo.
                    —Federico Garcia Lorca

From the cafe window I see a man
in a black trenchcoat trying to hail
a cab, snowflakes settling into his
slicked back hair like nesting sparrows
seeking safety, the sky crying its apologies.

EVEN IN NEW YORK, I LONG FOR NEW YORK

There should be nothing here I don't remember...
—Richard Blanco

I wander the night-streets of the Bronx
looking for my first home, that apartment
three stories above the crooked pavement,

spitting distance of Yankee Stadium, from which
we fled in the mid-nineties when the coke dealers
showed up on our block, that hard white

hitting our building like a baseball splintering
a window, where my cousin had to walk
the long blocks home from school

with house keys wedged between his fingers,
feigning brass knuckles whenever he got new
shoes, fists gleaming like heaps of broken glass

in sunlight— even Hermes could get
stomped out for his winged kicks here. Now
condos swell otherworldly into winter skies.

Arms of cranes and curved steel beams
rise from the ground, overarching the cityscape
like the hands of a tremendous puppeteer.

How bizarre. The building where I'd sit
on the fire escape that clung like brittle ivy,
and listen to the Yankee's game

while looking out at the stadium,
pounding fist into glove, dreaming
of a home run hit so far out of the park

that I'd be able to catch it— that building
may not even exist anymore. What is done
with the rubble of the replaced? I come to

Yankee Stadium, heart of the Bronx, dark as
anything tonight, for there is no baseball in winter.
But even this landmark, this birthmark

has been shifted, torn down
a few years ago and resurrected across the street
from where I stand,

feet planted in its original location—
just a park now, an unwalled
sea of jaded grass.

READING BASHO ON THE 2 TRAIN

Sequence of darkness
and then we emerge over
lightfields of the Bronx.

Faces of strangers
around me— silent, fallen
leaves swept on the train.

Doors slide open at
Freeman Station, the iced ground,
a haiku spoken:

As you leave the train,
please watch the gap between the
train and the platform.

MY DAD'S GUN

As a kid, I found my dad's gun
rusted and collecting dust behind
his framed diploma atop a bookshelf,

a summer afternoon spent at his house,
snooping around while he was away at work.
When I asked him about it he said

he was walking home from a party
in the Bronx when two shadows
jumped out of an alley, shoved

a gun in his face and demanded
he empty his pockets. But when
the streetlight's glow fell on his face

they noticed not the terror in his eyes
but rather his Caribbean curls
in a neat fro, his dark goosebumped skin,

and backed off, said *oh, sorry papo*.
One of them gave him a pat on the shoulder
before slipping back into the alley.

The next day he bought a gun,
unregistered, illegal, but wore it
everywhere he went just in case,

tucked into the waistline of his pants
even when he was taking classes
at City College and wore a full suit:

blue pants and jacket, white shirt,
red tie, black shoes he shined
every morning, trying to reflect

the success he knew was possible
in this country, and didn't really think
much of the gun after a while, until

one night, coming home from school
later than usual he found himself alone
in the compartment of an uptown train,

reading the newspaper. At the stop
before his, a band of five guys rushed
into the car, one of them hiding

something under his jacket, holding it
like a pregnant belly. My dad reached for his gun,
let his hand touch the cold metal

as the hand of a police officer
stopped the doors from closing,
stepped onto the train with his partner

and an old, silver haired woman who pointed
at everyone and confirmed with the officers
that yes, they were the ones who stole her purse.

As they put the guys in cuffs, one of the officers
glanced at my dad— who hadn't moved,
looking guiltier than anyone,

hand still frozen under his jacket,
sweat darkening his collar—
and shook his head as if to say

can you believe these guys? My dad
smiled back and bolted off the train,
thinking about deportation, or worse,

sprinting the few extra blocks home
in the cold, under streetlights casting
their long fingered shadows.

UNNOTICED

A pigeon slams into a building,
bounces off like bad check staving
off eviction, and crumples into a pile of
colorlessness on the crowded sidewalk.
So many feet stepping over and around,
so many eyes looking anywhere else.

TRANSIENTS WELCOME

for my grandfather

I walk down through Manhattan
from the Bronx, tracing the path
you must have taken in the hunt

for your first job in America,
some hotel on Park Avenue
you could never afford to stay in.

No money for a cab, you must
have walked the crowded city
in awe, more people on a single

street corner waiting to cross
then there were in the whole
Dominican Republic you left behind.

No money for the subway,
though maybe you considered
becoming a conductor,

despite the fear of being underground—
they must get paid well to wield
such huge machinery—

but you didn't come here to lead
people through darkness. Or did you?
Uptown now, where your son,

my father, will enroll in City College,
the first in the family to have his degree.
Uptown, where the trains emerge

Bronx bound or bent towards Queens,
or dive right into the very ground
you walk on below Manhattan

towards Brooklyn or far off Staten Island,
where another son is still locked up
in an asylum, Uncle Kiko in the embrace

of schizophrenia. He might be in the same
room you used to visit him in, I wouldn't know.
I don't visit him. I keep walking

just as you must have kept walking,
eyes bouncing around like a pinball—
the bars with strange names,

clothing stores, Chinese restaurants,
a post office, a donut shop with a bold
red sign that says *HOT & READY*

but not *HIRING*, and what do you know
about donuts anyway? You must have
walked past this same bodega in Washington Heights,

contemplated stopping for smokes
but there was no money for cigarettes
yet, and besides, you'll smoke twice as much

when your wife dies from lung cancer.
I have cousins in Washington Heights
that I would not recognize

if they were standing next to me on
this very same corner crossing
in the same direction but I keep walking

past coffee shops and food stands,
a farmers market, a pawn shop with a sign
that reads *WE BUY ANYTHING*

but not *HIRING*, and you don't have much
to sell anyway, anything of value
already gone to pay for the plane tickets,

the first months rent, food, a new
pair of shoes that lead you past
the length of Central Park. Did the acres

of autumned trees dishearten you,
leaves breaking from stems like
drifting days? Or had the decades

already taught that spring returns with
or without us? Midtown within sight
now, how the skyscrapers must have

floored you. The Empire State,
The Chrysler. Or perhaps you were
skeptical. *Rascacielo?*

How could the snow not come down
if their spires were truly piercing the clouds?
Did you consider going up

to the top floor of one to see
for yourself? But there wasn't much
time, the evening growing thin around you

as it does right now, the streetlights
coming to life, and an electric blue sign
down the block springs into view

in the window of a hotel, the words
TRANSIENTS WELCOME, and below
in red handwriting: *HELP WANTED.*

THINKING I SEE MY COUSIN BUSSING TABLES AT AN UPTOWN RESTAURANT

I order another beer
as he makes another round
just to get another look

but I still can't decide. It's been
so long since I've seen him
that I've forgotten how long it's been

since I've seen him. I try not to stare
as he wipes down table after table,
jotting orders in between. Even when

he takes the empty glasses from us
I can't look closely enough
to recognize the features of

the kid I once knew. I know he has
a chipped front tooth just like me—
his from a fight at a club, mine

from slipping on a basketball court—
but he doesn't smile as he works,
shuttling back and forth from

the kitchen to the floor to the bar
in his triangle of servitude.
No nametag on his blue uniform.

How to start that conversation?
I can't, though I remember
as a kid he had a nasty temper,

short fused and hotheaded,
so after almost two hours
as we leave, I don't leave

a tip, not a single dollar,
hoping he'll be so pissed off
he'll come out to confront me.

READING JAMES WRIGHT ON THE L TRAIN

Below the river, Brooklyn bound, I hold
his poems in one hand and the cold overhead
bar in the other, reading to myself on the crowded
evening train when a sudden heaving pulls me
from the text. I look up to see a young man
seated with his head lolling between his knees
to the rhythm of the train, Yankee cap pulled low
over his face, vomiting onto his shoes. Everyone
scatters to the adjacent compartments, lifting scarves
up to their noses as they exit. The vomit stretches
like an evening shadow down one end of the car
and I walk towards the other, lay down on a now
vacant bench. The train sways lightly, like a hammock.
Beneath a sun-marred window blossoming
with jewels of frost, I begin to read aloud.

NIGHTHAWKS OF THE 24-HOUR DONUT SHOPS

Midnight sun of the red blazing "O"
in the window, a beacon for wanderers
looking to escape the cold, or thrown-out
drunks trying to keep the night-talk alive
until morning arrives like an express train,
because the coffee refills here are free.
The undergrad who works the graveyard
shift lets them loiter, but has to remind
them every single night that if they want that
refill, they have to buy a cup of coffee first.

IN RESPONSE TO PEOPLE TRYING TO RENAME THE SOUTH BRONX "THE PIANO DISTRICT"

Of course they only see
the white keys— not the dark
veins that feed the heart
and sing.

O CHRISTMAS TREE

With my last two dollars I buy a coffee
to warm my ungloved hands, snow falling
soundlessly onto my upturned face

beneath the shadow of an enormous
Christmas tree, a skyscraper raised
overnight in midtown New York.

I try to fathom the flatbed it came to town in
from some far-northern Paul Bunyan
forest, and remember the eighteen wheelers

full of classic Fraser Firs and woolly Douglas trees
that I had to unload by hand when I worked
at a Home Depot in North Miami.

The trees were always stacked and netted
like body bags, from smallest to largest,
making it as difficult as possible to unload,

with the menacing twelve footers
still waiting in the back after hours
of dragging and lifting, dragging and lifting.

That winter was cold enough to send
the snowbirds home, temperatures dropping
to the upper 20's at night, and it was always cold

in those refrigerated trucks, though the sap
that oozed from the trees wasn't quite frozen
and so it would stick to my jeans, hoodies, gloves,

and that stupid orange apron, leaving me sap-
stained from head to aching feet. This was after
I graduated college, when I was so broke

I called out sick because I couldn't afford to put gas
 in the car that week to drive up to work and threw
up from eating ramen noodles for four days straight.

Never broke enough to pick up a penny
on the street though, knowing damn well
how worthless they are, not even pure copper—

even Abe is embarrassed, casting a sideways
stare to avoid eye contact. Those were the days
when I'd come home broken and stare

at my English degree hanging on the wall
like a crucifix that never answered a prayer.
I couldn't even afford a Christmas tree,

not even one of those shitty plastic tabletop ones,
and hated everyone who shopped at Home Depot
for theirs, having to cut the netting and twirl

tree after tree, only for them to say,
again and again: *Eh, I don't know.*
How about that big one in the back?

and I hated them even more, hoped the tree
they picked was full of spiders, even dead ones,
which often turned up in the frozen trucks

with their eight glazed eyes multiplying
the darkness, legs like dried pine needles.
Or maybe a stiff robin would drop down

on their gifts as their children hung lights
and angels from the branches, its beak
parted in yellowed silence. I always imagined

those creatures that turned up in the trailers
as sad, strange little immigrants fleeing
their homeland, smuggling themselves

in the trees, the trucks, their homes
destroyed but deciding to stay in them,
seeing the semi's license plate and dreaming

of Florida, that legendary place only mentioned
in the chatter of migratory birds, though I was
the only living thing ever inside the trailer,

sweeping out the dead critters into the piles
of pine needles, miniature funeral pyres. One night
it got so cold that I considered setting fire

to all the trees, watch them all light up brighter
than that giant one in New York. I didn't quit
that night— I just never came back, though I

stood out there a long time, broom in hand
fantasizing about the embers flickering
like tinsel, the smell of roasting pine needles.

And when the fire trucks finally arrive
and the police come and ask what happened
I'll wish them all a Merry fucking Christmas

as the fire jumps to the store front
and say this blaze is my gift
to myself— the only one I could afford.

THE YOUNG MEN ALONG THE BAR
ARE TOO TIRED EVEN TO DIE

after Phil Levine

We wear our work below our eyes.
How can someone so young be so tired?
my mother asks on voicemail, again.
But I am too tired to call back, too
tired to explain, too tired, even,
to walk home and close my eyes.
When's the last time the sun rose?
I don't remember. The only light
I know now is electric and hideous.
The ring on the bartop from my glass
is incomplete, broken like the moon
in the sky that could be in any season,
if I could bring myself to look up.

UPON ENCOUNTERING A STREET MURAL
OF SUPER MARIO, I THINK OF MY MOTHER

In his classic blue and red overalls,
poised to sprint as though he just robbed
the bodega on which he's spray painted,

he sends my mind racing back
to my seventh birthday when my mom
bought me an NES, the first Nintendo,

already outdated by two successors:
the Super Nintendo and the N64.
We found it at a flea market,

right in that sweet spot between
being recently discontinued
and becoming a collectors item.

It cost less than family lunch
at McDonalds (which was rare),
but still, I was stoked, especially

with the side-scrolling Mario,
blitzing through homework
and dinner to play every night,

jumping Goomba's and Koopa's,
bashing bricks, scouring for power ups,
always running, always running

and always that same message
at the end of every level:
your princess is in another castle.

Sometimes when I'd get home
from school I'd find my mom
in my room playing

before her night shift
at a SeaWorld gift shop
where she'd sell orca key chains,

tacky t-shirts, and glazed alligator
heads to dipshit tourists.
I'd wonder if she had been at it all day.

She got farther than I ever did
though I never thought much of it,
figured she was just trying to relax

before going to work— it didn't occur
to me that she was trying
to save herself.

MEDITATION ON HAPPINESS

I want to go through life
with the joy of a bus driver
riding through town in twilight,
catching all the green lights,
smiling softly as he hums along
to the radio and drives right by
all the bus stops, his display
glowing a single gleeful
orange word: *GARAGE*.

SELF PORTRAIT WITH A BEHEADED
SNOWMAN IN CENTRAL PARK

Across the fields of snow near an unfrozen
pond littered with ducks in remnant shades
of autumn, I see him: arms reaching to the bare
trees that gifted those limbs now raised
in despair. His head lies on its side a few steps
away, twig smile vertical, acorn eyes beady, dead
as the new moon. The park gives no answers:
the trees are quiet in the windless afternoon,
the still waters of the pond pretend to be frozen,
the ducks feign sleep, and the silent snow
has hidden all the footprints except my own.

SILENCE OVER THE SNOWY FIELDS

for Robert Bly

Through the plane's oval window: a harbor
bites into the mainland like a great blue dragon.
Heavy whiteness douses the landscape, forces
it to forget what it looks like, what it is, like
a mind that fails to recognize itself. Pin-
pricks of car headlights like cinder drifting
through the world, the remains of a once great
fire; dull azure of frozen lakes, visible in
shapeless patches beneath the falling snow
—the echoing nothingness of erasure—
the sound of it settling on the iced surface.

II

READING PO CHU-I ON MY BALCONY
ON A CLOUDY NIGHT

The moon must be out getting drunk
again. A week long binge of absence.
Or maybe just hiding a hangover,
drawing a curtain of stormclouds
to stop the neighbors from peeking.
When is the next new moon? I don't know
but I pour another glass of gas station wine
anyway. *I, too, am ugly* I say to the sky.
Join me— we could both use the company.

FOR THE MAN PRESSURE WASHING
THE GAS STATION NEXT DOOR AT 1 A.M.

Enough PSI to wake up the whole block,
to rival the airplanes idling across the street,
blast the concrete clean enough to reflect
the neon pink trim of the Airport Diner.
You might as well scrub at the light pollution
to reveal the stars. You're in for a long night.
No one will care. No one will notice.
I suppose you could say the same about
this poem. Don't worry, I wasn't sleeping anyway.

PERHAPS IT WASN'T SUCH A PERFECT DAY
FOR BANANAFISH

"Where is he?"
"On the beach."
"On the beach? By himself?"

—J.D. Salinger from *A Perfect Day for Bananafish*

Seagulls peck elegies in the warm evening sand.
Boats out on the water with sails like the long
feathers of sleeping swans. The breeze ghost-
writes the ocean's sorrow into tumbling waves.
A man stands in the foam staring at his feet,
hiding his toes in the cold froth. I lay Salinger's
Nine Stories in the bird-pocked sand, searching
through the glass of beach-side hotel windows
that amplify the sun's departure, ears perked
for the sound of a muffled gunshot.

DRIVING PAST LAKE TOHOPEKALIGA

Tilted trees suffer dusk
as I cruise along the winding
central Florida road, recalling

how my dad would pull over
whenever he spotted a turtle
crossing from grassland to asphalt—

perhaps mistaking the cars
for larger versions of themselves—
and return them to the waterside.

As a kid, I learned how to hold them
between thumb and forefinger,
or with two hands like a sandwich

with the bigger ones to avoid
their kicking, clawed feet, and how
to recognize the different species:

alligator snappers with their giant
beartrap jaws and huge heads,
too big to withdraw into their shells;

map turtles whose namesake comes
from markings along their bodies
that resemble contour lines;

red-ear sliders, named for the wound-
like markings on their faces,
streaks of feverish evening light.

Sometimes we would bring them home
and keep them in the kiddie pool
for a few days, though they always "escaped"

while I was at school, too young
to realize my dad had simply
taken them back to the lakeside.

This was so many years ago,
before the divorce, before my family
entered the new millennium in splinters.

These thoughts always seem to rise
on the drive from Miami
to Orlando to visit my dad,

who still lives in the same house
we left. I remember the first time
I went down to Miami—

it was in a U Haul
down a highway that splits
the sea of sawgrass.

There's a Buddhist ritual
that involves buying turtles
at food markets, turtles destined

for soup, and setting them free—
an unselfish act meant
to accrue good karma,

the turtles chosen over
chickens or lobsters
because they can outlive humans.

I never picked up my dad's habit,
though he still brings home
the occasional rescue.

I don't think he knows
about the ritual. I don't know
that he thinks much about karma,

I don't know if he knows
the name of the lake just south
of his home is *Tohopekaliga*,

which is a word in a language
older than any turtle he's ever found
and returned safely to that shore,

a word that translates
to something like a promise:
we will gather here together.

MEDITATION ON PATIENCE

Of patience, I know only
what sea turtles have taught me:
how they are born on lightless
beaches so the moon can serve
as a beacon to lure them
into the water; how they spend
their whole lives trying to swim
towards it, enamored, obsessed;
how they flap their forelimbs,
a vague recollection of flying—
the right movement in the wrong
medium, as if they knew how
to reach the moon in a former life
but now only remember the useless
persistent motions; how if you cut
one's heart out it would keep
beating in the pit of your palm,
recognizing the cold night air.

MY GRANDFATHER DIED OF PNEUMONIA

They found him in the courtyard
in the heart of the house staring up
at the slate of clouds, his pajamas
soaked through by rain down to his
wrinkled skin. They used to think
he'd sweat in his sleep. Every night
after everyone had gone to bed he'd go
out to the courtyard to count the stars,
and in the spring, when nightfall hitched
itself to storm clouds he'd count the drops
exploding against his pruning skin, rain
coming upon him like the days of his ninety
years, so many he'd lose count and return
the next night to start over. When asked why
he did it, hunched with age and wrapped
in a towel, he only smiled his toothless smile,
shivering with the thought of tomorrow.

JELLYFISH RAIN

Moon jellyfish amass
on the shores at summer's
end like memories.

Too fragile for this world,
they die simply from
the ocean's constant turmoil,

rolling them over and over.
Violet markings cover their bodies
like bright hieroglyphics,

a language no one can read,
perhaps explaining why
their home betrays them.

Or perhaps they're transcriptions
of their final thoughts.
The bay coughs them up

like phlegm, sticking to the sand
before slowly vanishing
from the shore and up into

the nothingness of the sky
dimming gray with clouds.
Nothing eats a dead jellyfish

except the heat of August.
Poised to return to Earth,
reincarnated, remembered—

rain is their afterlife,
falling back home
to the ocean's swell,

some mourning the beach
of their gravesite,
some falling on my head.

FOR THE WOMAN SELLING ROSES
ON MIAMI GARDENS DRIVE

I always see her on my drive home
at the light for the onramp to I-95,
one hand raised in the air, the petals

of her fingers spread out to show the price,
while the other hand holds
a bucket of roses to her chest, as if they bloomed

from her own body. And they are always
five dollars. On Monday, on Friday,
on the weekend, on Mother's Day, five dollars.

Always one hand fanned in the air,
always the roses clutched close to her heart,
holding them the way a red light holds traffic,

as though she doesn't want to part with them
but knows that she must, knows she carries
happiness or forgiveness for someone

she will never meet. Even on Valentine's Day,
when she could have charged more
to those fools who waited until the last minute.

Still only five dollars. Still one hand
open in the air, as if in order for her to raise the price,
she would have to put the roses down.

LIGHTS OUT, VAGABOND

Standing around with everyone else outside
of the now quiet bar after the power
goes out on the whole block: the darkness

a bouncer that won't let anyone back in,
the sign above the door that reads *Vagabond*
reduced to a dim tangle of shadow.

Looking around as my eyes adjust I see
a familiar face painted on the building's side:
a mural of Jack Kerouac with slicked back hair,

head turned slightly, just out of profile,
as if expecting someone to arrive from up
the road. I wonder what he's doing way out

here in South Florida, so far away from where
he was buried, so far away from where
his parents first arrived in America

from far off Canada, English a stranger
on their tongues, setting him off on his life-
long road trip through his homeland.

What happens to the soul of a wandering man?
I suppose not even death can keep his grip
on it, slipping through his bony fists,

and I imagine Jack in a black and shabby
suit and tie, matching dusty loafers, and an ever-
burning cigarette glued to his pale lips, dragging

his feet as he walks from Lowell to Miami,
following some long-abandoned railroad tracks
overgrown with weeds and wildflowers,

dandelions that dissipate in the night's wheezing
breath, where he looks up to the sound
of a howling wind, mistaking it for a train

coming up behind him, hoping to see
a light but always nothing there, silent thumbs
hooked in his worn-out belt loops— he never

hitches a ride anymore but stops at every
dive bar along the way to catch his breath,
and if there's no smoking allowed inside,

no one says a word to him about it. Looking
up at his face that keeps staring down the road,
I decide that if the lights come back on I'll buy

him a beer, pour it out into the middle of the street
until it fills the cracks in the asphalt,
and see in which direction it flows.

READING BUKOWSKI AT GRAMPS BAR

A small stained glass lamp in the corner
gives me light to read by. The bartender
keeps refilling my glass with liquid gold
like a goddamn alchemist and the promo
girls are giving out free Jameson. My tab
is open and I don't bother to check the time.
There's a blonde eyeing me from across
the tottering room with her bluebird eyes
and I'm tempted to smash the little lamp
over my own head, scoop up the glass
pieces in quivering hands, and offer
them to her as the shards of my heart.

RAT IN THE CRAWL SPACE

It isn't raining tonight, so I know
it's you scurrying about above me,
your footfalls a soft drizzle keeping
sleep at bay, and again I am the sad
child with the storm cloud over his head.
Normally, I would hate you, consider
spending this sleepless time driving
to Wal-Mart for rat traps or worse,
those cubes that coagulate your blood
into something thicker than the cough syrup
I'm trying to ween off of. But tonight
I'm too tired to hate you. Tonight
I wish you only peace, knowing
that if you sleep, then maybe I will too.

READING JOSE MARTI AT CHURCHILL'S

I order a *Cuba Libre* even though I know
they don't serve Cuban rum, and watch
the punk band on stage sweat music into
the crowd that begins to form a giant maelstrom
of wailing limbs, heads snapping back and forth
to the thunderstorm of double bass drums,
guitars electrifying the air thick with smoke, voices
rising like balloons slipped from a hand. I find
myself nodding along, a buoy in premonitory waters,
surrounded by flailing strangers that seem to be
reaching out to me, for me. I pocket my glasses, use
Versos Sencillos as a coaster, and charge into the eye.

AT MIAMI JAI-ALAI AND CASINO

A debt of heavy storm clouds accrues
overhead, and I duck inside to avoid
the rain come to collect my warmth.

A one dollar beer, a two dollar bet,
I sit down among the other broke men,
a crowd that wouldn't fill a poetry reading,

who cheer and heckle in Spanish
and Creole, watch the players
jump, catch, twirl, throw, the pelota

slamming with thunder against
the faded fronton— the sound
of a dollar won, a dollar lost.

They dream their bet will pay off big
but regret not buying a bus pass instead
as they walk home hatless through the rain.

I fold my ticket into a tiny paper boat,
concentrate on the point of the bow,
the thickness of the starboard, picture it

floating along the gutter, staying upright
despite the rain's onslaught until it reaches
the open ocean. Suddenly, applause:

I look up, boat in hand— the game
has ended and I've forgotten
who I bet on.

READING EMILY DICKINSON IN LINE
AT THE BODEGA JUST AFTER 2 A.M.

After reading several poems, I realize
the line hasn't moved at all: the woman
in front of me in a pale blue raincoat
seems to be counting the cigarette packs
behind the counter, as if she's always
wanted to smoke and this may be her
last chance. The six pack in my basket
is getting warm. No one is behind me.
The cashier, thankful for the lapse,
rests her chin on her hand and snores.

POST HURRICANE, MIAMI

I step out into the unseasonal chill
that fills the violent space left behind,
watch the stillness of flood water

in the streets of this city reduced
to nameless shapes in darkness,
wind chimes hanging from the doorframe,

silent now in the aftermath like the hollow
bones of birds they so resemble. I tilt
back another beer until I'm looking up,

raise the bottle to my eye and blink
away a few stray drops: a crude telescope
to view the stars, blurred and imperfect

as though crafted by my own drunken hands.
Waiting when the sun sets on downed
power lines and ruptured transformers,

they hold no ill will towards us
for creating replacements, don't hesitate
to return when their shoddy imitators fail.

Even dead stars give us their light.
One twinkles occasionally and I recall
looking up at the sky through the window

of my childhood room, catching the shimmer
and making a wish for another week
without school, or for the flood waters

to recede so I could play outside.
But now I know that a twinkling star is just
a satellite, another man-made thing

not quite as far away as the stars, though far enough
to see the world as a whole. Far enough
to see the hurricane somewhere out

in the Atlantic, spinning itself into nothingness,
dissipating under its own destructive power.
Far enough to see who still has electricity

and who doesn't, and yet far enough to not see
me standing in my doorway. Far enough
to not see itself reflected in the water. I toss

the bottle into the flooded street, watch
the ripples, the way the movement makes
the star's reflections waver, twinkle

all becoming satellites, watchers, until a new
flickering catches my eye,
a glow emerging from the storefront

of a fortune teller across the street: candles being lit,
one after another, and soon I can make out
the silhouette of a woman shuffling tarot cards

on a tabletop, their worn out edges slapping one another
with the silence of leaves drifting down
from rattled branches to rain-soaked pavement

again and again, as if waiting for something
or someone, the candle wax melting into puddles.
I wade across the flooded street and knock

against the window, press both palms against the glass:
one to show I have nothing with which to pay,
the other for her to read anyway.

SELF PORTRAIT WITH MOTHS AFTER RAIN

Moths stumble through dusk, descending
towards the glow of a glimmering lamppost
mirrored in the water of a rain-filled pothole.

MAGIC CITY RUSE

Miami Beach burns with the insatiable
ego of a galaxy, bright enough to refuse
admittance to any stars in the night sky.

I walk its neoned grid, past hotels
and restaurants, sidewalk cafes that pulse
with radioactivity like the lanes

of a pinball machine, or a Twilight Zone
town that's stuck in Christmas time,
crowds made up of everyone

I've ever hated, talking too loudly
or stepping on my shoes, or both
as I trudge to a poetry reading.

Awful music spews into the street
and I think this is how whales must feel
about sonar, how it drives them

crazy enough to try and defy evolution
and crawl onto land, though not crazy
enough to beach themselves here.

To distract myself, I search for the motel
from *Scarface*, where Tony escapes
with the blood of his chainsawed friend

splattered all over him in a drop top
speeding down Ocean Drive.
Tony, dead facedown in his living

room fountain, like Gatsby
laid out poolside. What is it
with dreamers dying bloody

by the water? Crossing 13th
I'm almost run over by a Ferrari,
red as the stop sign it ignored.

I take solace in the fact that scientists
believe Miami will soon be swallowed
by the Atlantic like a child gulping

his vegetables whole so he won't
have to taste them, and picture
the neon being extinguished, this stupid

Ferrari encrusted with shit-colored barnacles.
The idiot behind the wheel leans
into the horn, the blare masking

his curses and mixing with the nonsense
conversations floating up from the crowded
sidewalk, the garbage pop blitzing out

of cafe speakers, hostesses yelling out
drink specials in frenzied desperation—
but beneath all that, I hear another sound

that trembles from across the street: waves
pawing at the shore, the ocean mumbling
its desire for the day that it will drown out

all the lights and noise for good,
and let the stars return to this night sky,
O, let it be soon. Let it be soon.

THE WORLD AND EVERYTHING IN IT

Night drive through Miami,
I think the sky a dream
not yet starred by bullets.

FOURTH OF JULY

Children point to a single
red light drifting above
the city— they do not know
the words "Chinese lantern."
From my window I see
the rain coming home,
so I walk to the bar. Smoke
from the evening's fireworks
lingers like the morning star
after a sleepless, burnt out night.
I sit at the far corner of the bar,
away from the door. Grief
from the jukebox: love songs
that rattle the night's stillness
in the absence of explosions.

PISSING ON THE LAWN OF A FORECLOSED HOME

A chorus of frogs petitions for the moon
to roll out from beneath the clouds
as I make a pit-stop on my stagger home—
I'm not going to make it and I know
there will be no one peeking through
the grimy window, no light flicked on
in response to a drunk in the yellowing yard.
What's another patch of dead grass anyway?
I do my best to get every drop onto
the ugly white sign but fail miserably.
That gold coin of a moon appears, fat
and disapproving, and I think maybe
the frogs are crying for someone else.

READING TU FU IN THE MORNING

Cold pizza for breakfast
again, another night wasted
in sleeplessness. *I live
like a parasite— happily,*
says Tu Fu, and I think
I have the first part down.
Overhead, the moon's out,
heirloom of the night, a light
someone forgot to turn off.

WHEN LIFE GIVES YOU LEMONS

Sell them on the corner of 135th and Douglas
in green netted sacks for ten dollars a dozen,
hold them in each hand like heavy boleadoras.
Learn to hate the rain, the way it sends you
to cover under the bus stop like a grounded
child damned to his room, each drop a lost sale.
Learn to hate the green lights that urge
drivers to pass you by without a second glance.
Learn to hate even the thought of lemonade
as you sweat and sweat in the bowels of summer
under the relentless sun you've learned to hate
so well, the way it leans its tremendous weight
all day long into the back of your neck.

THE BOTTOMS OF MY SHOES ARE CLEAN
FROM WALKING IN THE RAIN

after Jack Kerouac

Cashless and bus-pass-less, the sun
plows through spent clouds as I walk
home, relieved for the chance
to dry after the sudden rainstorm,
brief and brutal as a mugging.
I'm doing my best to be happier.
My socks are soaked but my shoes
are clean, and those shapeless
greens shooting up raised fists
from the cracked sidewalk, fed
by this same rain I wear so heavily—
who's to say that's not a garden?

POEM WRITTEN AT 3 A.M.

after Donald Justice

Excepting the Airport Diner
on the outskirts
the city of Miami Springs
at 3 A.M.
was dark but
for my desk lamp
and down on
36th street
the headlights
of someone
sleepless
or fleeing
at seventy
as I looked down
thinking
this poem is for whoever
broke that darkness
however briefly.

AMERICAN NIGHT, AMERICAN MORNING

Fuck a dollar and a dream.
    —Biggie Smalls

When I can't sleep I go
up to the rooftop
of my apartment building

and watch the man who sleeps
on the bus stop bench
across the street, brown by birth

or sun. I want to ask him
How do you do it?
From here I can see a lottery

jackpot billboard off the highway
mid-update, so that it currently reads
WIN 0 MILLION.

I was born in the city
that never sleeps so perhaps
insomnia is my birthright.

Even in Miami, the New York
air must have stuck to the inside
of my lungs like cigarette tar,

directing my luck towards
noise and lights. Sometimes
it's the cops who always

pull people over in front
of my apartment at every hour
with their howling sirens,

sometimes it's the jet planes
across the street, rattling
my windows with takeoff,

their overcaffeinated pilots
dreaming of sleep too.
Sometimes it's the stack

of mail on my nightstand
from the doctor's office,
credit card companies, Sallie

Mae, the IRS, all unopened,
collecting dust instead
of collecting from me.

The things that weigh me down
must have pressed me into sleep
right on the rooftop because I wake

to sparrows hopping about
my head, the highway singing
its blues of passing traffic.

The sun hangs in the sky
out of reach, revealing
the unfamiliar faces

at the bus stop, how much
the lottery is now, how late
I am for work.

WHEN EVERYONE LEAVES FOR OTHER PLANETS
I WILL STAY IN THE ABANDONED CITY
DRINKING A LAST GLASS OF BEER

after Jorge Teillier

Even the bartender has left, maybe landing
a gig on the dark side of Mars. I put Rocket Man
on the jukebox, laugh along with no one,
taking small sips in the dim light. Outside, a breeze
runs through emptied streets like a pack of stray dogs.
The stars howl their light into the ether, try to reach
each other. They only look close together
from this great distance. The record ends
and I let it spin on, static filling the room like smoke,
the soundtrack of this hollowness. I put down
the empty glass, tap the bar top, and say out loud
put it on my tab. Then I cut the lights to the last
bar on Earth, and lock the door behind me.

Acknowledgements

Grateful acknowledgement is made to the following literary magazines where some of these poems first appeared, sometimes in earlier forms:

Academy of American Poets: "Before Snowfall"
Best New Poets 2016: "Meditation on Patience" reprint
The Boiler Journal: "Post Hurricane, Miami", "Silence Over the Snowy Fields"
Boston Accent: "Jellyfish Rain", "Reading Tu Fu in the Morning"
Breakwater Review: "In Response to People Trying to Rename the South Bronx 'The Piano District'", "Looking Down from Atop the Empire State Building", "Tulips in Winter"
Cha: An Asian Literary Journal: "Reading Basho on the 2 Train"
Dirty Chai: "For the Man Pressure Washing the Gas Station Next Door at 1 A.M."
Duende: "Reading James Wright on the L Train"
ELKE "A Little Journal": "When Everyone Leaves for Other Planets, I Will Stay in the Abandoned City, Drinking a Last Glass of Beer"
Fjords Review: "Meditation on Patience"
Gulf Coast: "Magic City Ruse"
The Grief Diaries: "Driving Past Lake Tohopekaliga"
Indianola Review: "Reading Lorca At Union Square"
The National Poetry Review: "Even in New York, I Long for New York"
Off the Coast: "Reading Emily Dickinson at the Bodega Just After 2 A.M.", "Reading Jose Marti at Churchill's"
O, Miami: And Justice for All: "Poem Written at 3A.M."
Ofi Press: "When Life Gives You Lemons"
Origins Literary Journal: "American Night, American Morning", "For the Woman Selling Roses on Miami Gardens Drive", "Meditation on Happiness", "O Christmas Tree", "Transients Welcome"
PANK Magazine: "The World and Everything in It", "The Young Men Along the Bar are Too Tired Even to Die"
Poetry Quarterly: "My Grandfather Died of Pneumonia"
Portland Review: "Reading Keats at Freeman Station"
Prelude: "Thinking I See My Cousin Bussing Tables at an Uptown Restaurant"
Saw Palm: "The Bottoms of My Shoes are Clean from Walking in the Rain"
The Shallow Ends: "I Know You Love Manhattan But You Should Look up More Often"

Sliver of Stone: "At Miami Jai-Alai and Casino", "Perhaps it Wasn't Such a Perfect Day for Bananafish"

Tinderbox Poetry Journal: "My Dad's Gun", "Nighthawks of the 24-Hour Donut Shops"

Two Peach: "Rat in the Crawl Space"

Tupelo Quarterly: "A View of the Statue of Liberty from the Brooklyn Bridge"

Vending Machine Press: "Lights Out, Vagabond", "Self Portrait With a Beheaded Snowman in Central Park", "Self Portrait With Moths After Rain"

Washington Square: "Reading Bukowski at Gramps Bar"

Whiskey Island: "Reading Po Chu-I on My Balcony on a Cloudy Night"

Glass Poetry Press: "Upon Encountering a Street Mural of Super Mario, I Think of My Mother"

Yes Poetry: "Pissing on the Lawn of a Foreclosed Home"

Thank you to John Gosslee, Andrew Sullivan, and everyone at C&R Press for believing in my work; thank you to Denise Duhamel and Campbell McGrath for their support, wisdom, and guidance all these years; thank you to Julie Marie Wade and everyone at Florida International University's MFA; thank you to Peg Boyers and everyone at the New York State Summer Writers Institute; thank you to my dear friends Marci Calabretta Cancio-Bello, Paul Christiansen, Carlie Hoffman, and Nadra Mabrouk for their honesty, advice, and feedback at (almost) any hour.

OTHER C&R PRESS TITLES

FICTION

Ivy vs. Dogg
by Brian Leung

A History of the Cat In Nine Chapters or Less
by Anis Shivani

While You Were Gone
by Sybil Baker

Spectrum
by Martin Ott

That Man in Our Lives
by Xu Xi

SHORT FICTION

Meditations on the Mother Tongue
by An Tran

The Protester Has Been Released
by Janet Sarbanes

ESSAY AND CREATIVE NONFICTION

Immigration Essays
by Sybil Baker

Je suis l'autre: Essays and Interrogations
by Kristina Marie Darling

Death of Art
by Chris Campanioni

POETRY

Negro Side of the Moon
by Early Braggs

Holdfast
by Christian Anton Gerard

Ex Domestica
by E.G. Cunningham

Collected Lies and Love Poems
by John Reed

Imagine Not Drowning
by Kelli Allen

Les Fauves
by Barbara Crooker

Tall as You are Tall Between Them
by Annie Christain

The Couple Who Fell to Earth
by Michelle Bitting

CHAPBOOKS

Cuntstruck by Kate Northrop
Relief Map by Erin Bertram
Love Undefined by Jonathan Katz
A Hunger Called Music: A Verse History in Black Music
by Meredith Nnoka

CPSIA information can be obtained
at www.ICGtesting.com
Printed in the USA
FSHW04n1627160418
46819FS